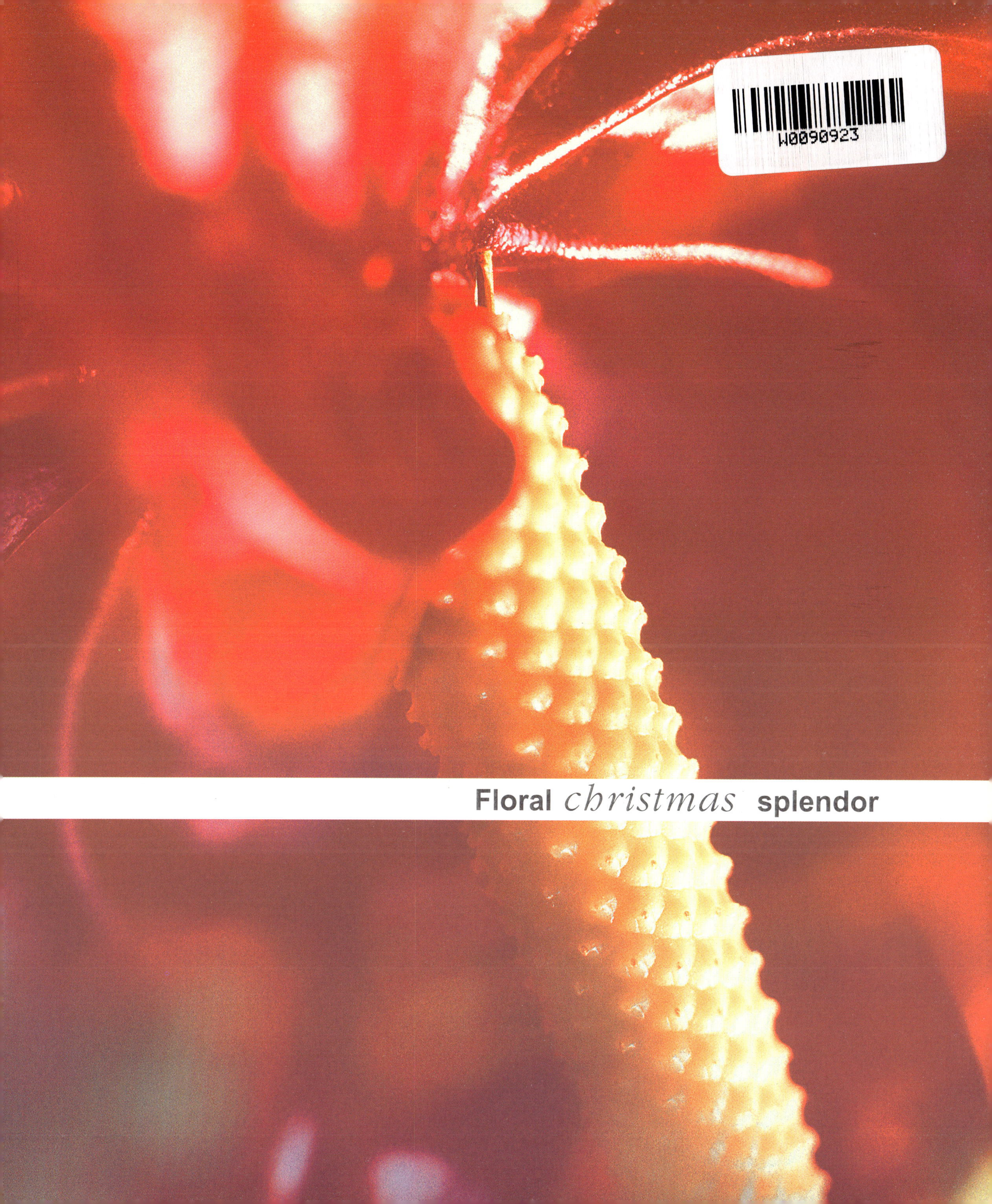

Floral *christmas* **splendor**

contents

35

79

13

55

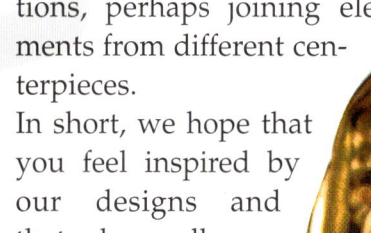

There is nothing quite so inspiring as working with Nature's raw materials to create something personalized and new.

With just a handful of basic ingredients –such as plants, flowers (Mother Earth's natural works of art) and perhaps some colorful ribbon and wire– you can effortlessly create fantastic floral arrangements and wreaths to fill your home with a warm and festive atmosphere during the Christmas holiday season.

In deciding upon the myriad of Christmas arrangements possible, we have chosen a wide variety of styles (ranging from romantic to whimsical to classic) all of which are surprisingly simple to put together.

But above all, we have tried to compile an inspiring collection, one that will serve as a springboard to creating your own unique style of wreath or centerpiece.

We hope that, once you are familiarized with these basic ingredients, you feel free to branch off in new directions, perhaps joining elements from different centerpieces.

In short, we hope that you feel inspired by our designs and that, above all, you have fun with them!

technique

Type of composition: Decorative symmetric, pyramid.
Materials used: Grass / Osier wands / Moss / Cinnamon / Roses / Wheat / Broom / Copper wire / Poppies / Galax

Using osier wands, broom and grass, build and bind the body of the composition in an elongated pyramid shape. The other materials can be arranged around and inserted into this central core, reinforcing the pyramid shape. Galax, poppies or roses can be included to enhance the composition, although they will need to be replaced during the season.

compositions

christmas

Style: Parallel decorative
Technique: Foam
Color scheme: Contrasting
Size: 35 cm x 28 cm
Tendency: Clustered

This parallel composition uses a wine press for a base, and is formed by three complementary clusters centered around irises, candles and a white tulip. Red accents placed selectively throughout the arrangement provide the desired festive tone. The broad base is especially appropriate for this parallel combination; while the variety of components used does nothing to impair the definition and clarity of the overall composition.

Ingredients

1 Iris germanica / iris 2 Red rose 3 Ilex aquifolium / Common holly 4 Fatsia japonica / Fatsia
5 Asparagus meyeri / Asparagus 6 Tulipa gesnerana / Tulip 7 Platycladus orientalis / Platycladus
8 African greenery

christmas

Style: Classical
Technique: Foam
Color scheme: Warm
Size: 100 cm x 70 cm
Tendency: Enveloping

With plants native to both cold climates (such as the fir) and warm (the vriesia), this composition exudes warmth and freshness. A similar contrast is created between the poinsettia, which prefers sunlight and heat, and the papyrus, which thrives in damp, shady areas. Make sure to give each element ample space, thereby granting each one an important role of its own.

Ingredients

1. Euphorbia pulcherrima / Poinsettia 2. Cyperus papyrus / Papyrus 3. Vriesia favoriet / Vriesia 4. Phormium tenax / New Zealand hemp 5. Abies procera / Noble fir 6. Camelia japonica / Common camelia 7. Lilium Star Gaze / Lily 8. Cotoneaster horizontalis / Rock Cotoneaster 9. Arecastrum romanzofianum / Arecastrum 10. Salix matsudana tortuosa / Contorted willow

christmas

Style: Classical half-moon
Technique: Foam
Color scheme: Contrasting
Size: 90 cm x 40 cm
Tendency: Semitransparency

A festive composition for a luxurious setting, combining a classical line and shape with elements typical of the season, from the most sophisticated (such as the gold-painted edges of the rose petals) to the simplicity of boughs draped with lichen and the ever-popular mistletoe, holly and spruce. Be sure to reinforce the top of the foam with plenty of wire mesh, otherwise the bulkier branches might split the base.

 **Ingredients**

 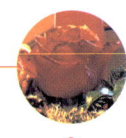   

1   2   3   4   5

1. Rose (orange) 2. Rose (red) 3. Common holly 4. Picea nobilis / Spruce 5. Boughs with lichen

christmas

Style: Formal
Technique: Collage and foam
Color scheme: Contrasting
Size: 120 cm.
Tendency: Clustered units

With the flower pot firmly attached to the tripod, form well-defined clusters that are brought together in the same arrangement, yet without interfering with each other. The central cluster is dominated by a magnolia, the beauty and aroma of which permeate the surroundings. Ribbons in old gold add a stately tone. Magnolias in bloom are far from common at this time of year, and it is well worth creating a whole composition to mark the rarity of the find.

 **Ingredients**

1   2   3   4   5

Asparagus setaceus / Asparagus   Magnolia soulangiana / Saucer magnolia
Triticum triticale / Wheat   Gourds   Ribbon

christmas

Style: Classical
Technique: Pinned and wired
Color scheme: Monochrome
Size: 60 cm x 140 cm
Tendency: Clustered

The tripod's style and shape imbue the composition with a note of modernity. The lower part must be densely worked to conceal the foam that holds the materials, wich are a mixture of dried and fresh floral elements and Christmas decorations. The anthurium can be used as the centerpiece to draw the elements together, or as an accent suspended from the arrangement.

 **Ingredients**

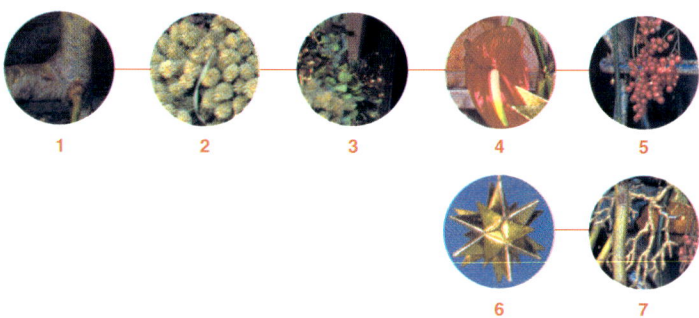

1. Salix matsudana tortuosa / Contorted willow 2. Phalaris arundinaceae / Red canary grass
3. Hydrangea macrophylla / French hydrangea 4. Anthurium favoriet 5. Schinus molle / Pepper tree
6. Christmas decorations 7. Decorative branches

christmas  composition

Style: Classical
Technique: Foam
Color scheme: Complete range
Size: 150 cms.
Tendency: Layered transparency

The main aim here is to bring together a wide variety of materials into a single composition, regardless of whether they are fresh, dried or artificial. Each element is shown off to its best advantage, unobstructed by its neighbors, enabling the viewer to enjoy each part and the whole simultaneously. The result is formally loose, with unique appeal, singular luminosity and a fine balance between its classical form and modern finish.

 **Ingredients**

1 2 3 4 5

6 7

1. Abies procera / Noble fir 2. Protea compacta / Protea 3. Guindillas / Chili peppers 4. Artificial fruit 5. Branch
6. Ribbon 7. Raffia

christmas

Style: Traditional
Technique: Kenzan
Color: Contrasting
Size: 110 cm x 40 cm
Tendency: Clustered

This composition brings together all the typical Christmas elements, in their variety of shapes and colors: wreaths, pine cones, mistletoe, balls, greens, golds and reds. These simple, traditional elements provide infinite variations at the service of creativity, as they are easy to handle, have clean lines, and exert a strong and immediate appeal. The result is an ideal accessory for shop windows, buffets, foyers and similar display spaces.

 **Ingredients**

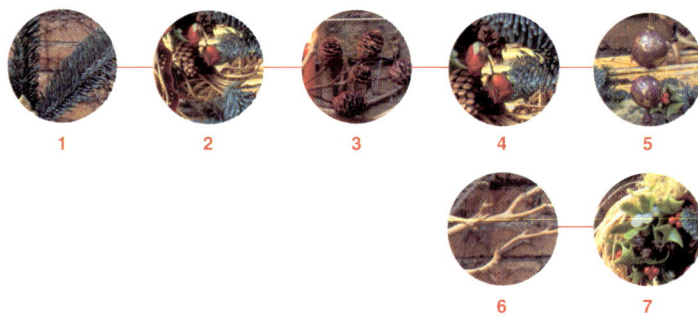

1. Abies procera / Noble fir 2. Wickerwork wreath 3. Pine cones 4. Roses (dried) 5. Christmas balls
6. Lagestroemia indica / Lagestroemia 7. Artificial berries

composition

christmas

Style: Formal
Technique: Collage
Color scheme: Complete range of earth tones and complementary colors
Size: 120 cm
Tendency: Transparency

Once the wicker ball is well attached to the cylinder, create all the points of interest within it, making sure not to overburden it, as this would destroy the transparency effect. First work the base and then arrange the love-lies-bleeding and the callas to harmonize the surface. This is a very particular approach to the half-moon composition, with a highly dominant center.

 **Ingredients**

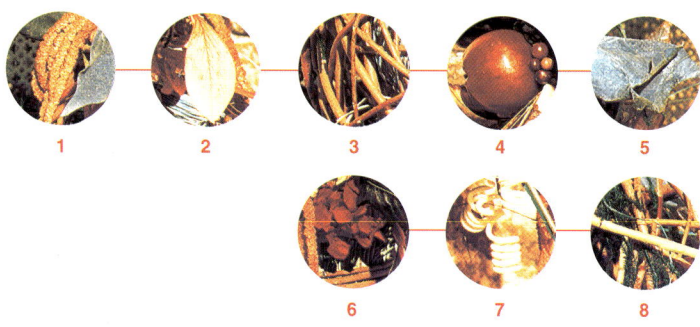

1 Amaranthus caudatus / Love-lies-bleeding (dyed) 2 Nasturtion (treated) 3 Wicker ball
4 Fruits (artificial) 5 Callas (artificial) 6 Hydrangeas (artificial, in various colors) 7 Decorations 8 Greenery

christmas

Style: Linear
Technique: Foam
Color scheme: Contrasting
Size: 70 cm x 50 cm
Tendency: Structured

A very interesting composition, a harmonious blend between a classical and an avant-garde line, and between linear and structural definitions. It consists of a centerpiece in a halfmoon shape standing on a conical dry foam base that features a structure in dogwood vine. Spectacular projections strike a balance with the center, and adhere to a general triangular tendency.

Ingredients

1. Rosa canina / Dog rose (hips) 2. Rosa Dallas / Rose (red, petals)
3. Anthurium favoriet / Anthurium 4. Hedera helix / English ivy 5. Salix matsudana tortuosa / Contorted willow
6. Artificial apples 7. Cornus alba / Dogwood 8. Brash wire mesh 9. Gold leaf aged with mastic
10. Ginkgo biloba / Ginkgo

christmas

Style: Traditional pyramidal
Technique: Foam
Color scheme: Range of ochres
Size: 80 cm x 40 cm
Tendency: Clustered

A visual interplay somewhere between a composition and a miniature classical Christmas tree, between vegetative and vertical, that can be arranged differently depending on the feeling one wishes to convey. A harmonious balance is struck between the clusters that adorn it, thanks to the right color combination: dull ochres, gold ribbon, greens, browns and the ruddy tone of the hydrangea blend perfectly with the hues of the pine cones and walnut shells.

 **Ingredients**

1 | 2 | 3 | 4 | 5

1. Abies procera / Noble fir 2. Bows 3. Hydrangea (treated) 4. Walnuts 5. Pine cones

wreaths

christmas

Style: Formal
Technique: Bound
Color scheme: Autumnal
Size: 60 cm diameter
Tendency: Clustered

A pre-Advent decoration with an autumnal look, belonging to the beginning of winter and the first hints of festive atmosphere. The wreath, made with fallen leaves from the garden, recalls sunny days in the shade of the fir tree, the perfume of the magnolia exuding a fruity aroma, the freshness of the ivy and walls covered in Virginia creeper.

Ingredients

1. Picea nobilis / Spruce   2. Hedera helix / English ivy   3. Parthenocissus tricuspicata / Ampelopsis, Virginia creeper

4. Ceratonia siliqua / Carob   5. Saucer magnolia / Magnolia   6. Castanea sativa / Sweet chestnut

7. Buxus sempervirens / Box   8. Paulownia tormentosa / Paulownia

christmas wreaths

Style: Format classical rustic
Technique: Pinned
Color scheme: Contrasting
Size: 40 cm diameter
Tendency: Textural clusters

Start by making clusters of fir and moss. The former is toned down by more tranquil materials, and the hues of the latter are intensified by a variety of materials. It is a wreath made up of a mixture of dried and fresh natural elements, and can be given a sculptural finish by adding flourishes of sarsaparilla vine.

 **Ingredients**

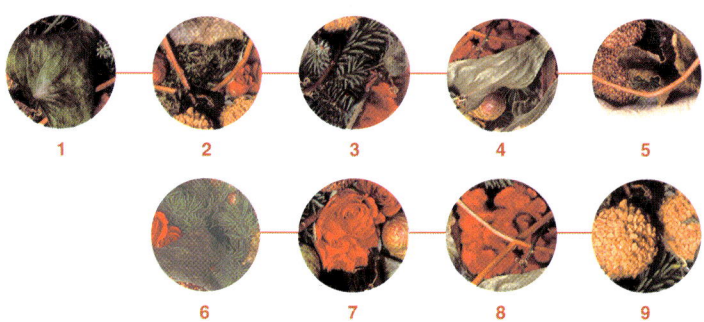

1. Galax aphylla / Galax 2. Moss (dried) 3. Abies masjoanni / Fir

4. Smilax aspera / Sarsaparilla 5. Salix matsudana tortuosa / Contorted willow

6. Asparagus umbellatus midiocladus / Asparagus 7. Rosa Red Ace / Rose (red)

8. Celosia cristata / Cockscomb 9. Balls of seeds

Style: Classical
Technique: Woven
Color scheme: Monochrome
Size: 50 cm diameter
Tendency: transparency

A simple, easy-to-construct circular figure made of a number of tough stems interwoven and covered with a wide variety of foliage. Layers of herbaceous stems are built up to conceal the inflexibility of the woody internal structure. The monochrome scheme of the whole is enriched by an array of plants, granting an overall harmonious effect.

 **Ingredients**

1 2 3 4 5

6 7

1.Hedera helix / English ivy 2.Cupressus sempervirens / Italian cypress 3.Magnolia soulangiana / Saucer magnolia
4.Schinus molle / Pepper tree 5.Balls of moss 6.Asparagus treeferm / Asparagus
7.Clematis vitalba / Travelle's joy

christmas

Style: Formal
Technique: Bound and pinned
Color scheme: Analogous
Size: 140 cm diameter
Tendency: Textural

Symbolic representation of the Star of Bethlehem using dry foam. The two straw-lined wreaths are covered with platycladus and the star is decorated with a textural creation in a free style. The materials are clustered to generate points of interest with their color. The piece is completed by recreating the work in the smaller wreath. The analogous harmony is far-reaching and transmits a sensation of depth and richness.

🌹 Ingredients

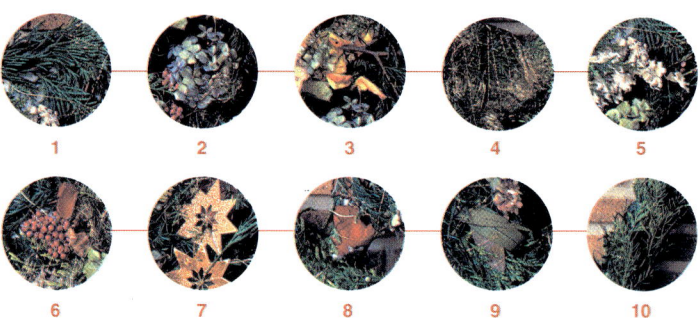

1. Platycladus orientalis 2. Hydrangea macrophylla 3. Rose (two-colored) 4. Coiled metal wire 5. Lichen
6. Schinus molle / pepper tree 7. Decorative stars 8. Rose (red petals) 9. Eucalyptus globulus / Cider gum
10. Asparagus sprengeri / Asparagus

christmas

Style: Formal
Technique: Collage
Color scheme: Monochrome
Size: 30 cm
Tendency: Woven

A minimalist piece in which the fully visible woven wicker base takes on an important role in its own right. The only adornment in this wreath is the grouping at the top, made of materials glued together to form a single central cluster. The ribbons help to create a linear perspective, softening the compact character of the composition. All the materials are natural.

 **Ingredients**

1 2 3 4 5

1. Wreath base in white wickerwork   2. Norway spruce cone   3. Rose   4. Helipterum   5. Mexican hats on stem

christmas

Style: Classical
Technique: Collage (glued)
Color scheme: Neutral
Size: 40 cm diameter
Tendency: Rustic clusters

A creative composition made out of pasta arranged in clusters to form a pleasant mosaic with a very everyday charm. The three rosettes attached to the cascading ribbon lend a festive air, lengthen the shape of the piece and provide it with an elegant finish. The warm tones easily adapt to the surroundings.

 **Ingredients**

1

1.Pasta

christmas

Style: Formal
Técnica: Collage
Colour: Natural
Size: 30 cms. diameter
Tendency: Sobriety

A treatment far removed from snowy alpine connotations, focusing instead on elements characteristic of the seashore, this arrangement displays its own unique brand of Christmas authenticity and sobriety. Carefully chosen shells and conches, bundles of willow cuttings and raffia tassels are all that adorn this wickerwork wreath, which emanates a beauty of its own without the need of further ornamentation.

 **Ingredients**

1   2   3   4   5

1.Wickerwork wreath   2.Raffia   3.Contorted willow   4.Conches   5.Shells

christmas

Style: Decorative
Technique: Bound and pinned
Color scheme: Analogous
Size: 40 cm. diameter
Tendency: Vegetative

This wreath emanates subtlety and natural-ness, thanks to its fluid, organic form. The sinuous lines of the stand give it extra depth and become part of a more general whole, thus creating an interesting, unified composition. Small decorative touches adorn the ends of the twigs without being too obvious. The right combination of dried materials and fresh flowers and plants helps to balance the originality of the whole. The berries add a festive note.

Ingredients

1. Lilium Casablanca / lily 2. Asparagus sprengeri / Asparagus 3. Salix atrocinerea / Common sallow
4. Rosa Evelyn Fison / Rose (profusely flowering) 5. Schinus molle / Pepper tree 6. Log 7. Fabric
8. African greenery 9. Hydrangea macrophylla / French hydrangea

christmas

Style: Classical
Technique: Overlapping with stitching
Color scheme: Contrasting monochrome
Size: 50 cm. diameter
Tendency: Bunched

Construct a framework with galvanized wire as a base, to which the floral materials are to be attached. The fir cuttings are all cut to the same length and then stitched to the base; by overlapping them like scales the wire is always concealed by the next cutting. If the wreath is to be hung, the inside and back must also be well worked to ensure that the volume is balanced.

Ingredients

 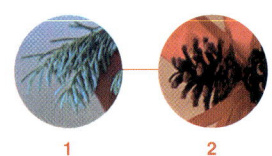

1

2

1. Abies masjoanni / Fir   2. Pinus nigra / Black pine

christmas

Style: Formal
Technique: Bound
Color scheme: Monochrome
Size: 60 cm. diameter
Tendency: Simplicity

While wreaths almost invariably belong to the category of formal arrangements, an interpretation such as this one, which displays little more than the basic shape, clearly merits a different approach. The work, in this case, is no more than a synthesis, a metaphor representing the passing of time through the harvesting of the fruits of the earth, the winter stores, the living earth that lies beating under the moss. An expressive compendium of time, laden with symbolic elements.

 **Ingredients**

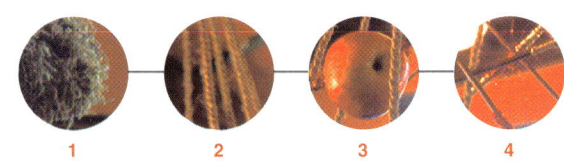

1 2 3 4

1 Moss   2 Esparto cord   3 Apples   4 Salix viminalis / Common osier (with decorations)

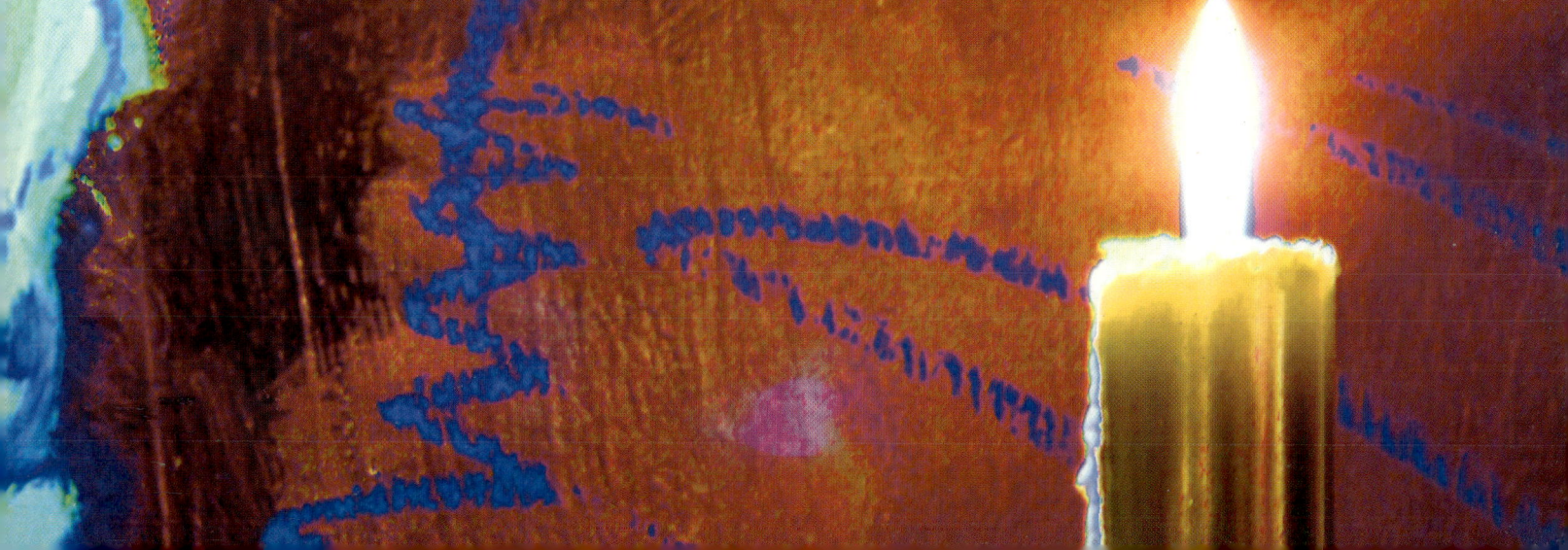

centerpieces

christmas

Style: Classical
Technique: Foam
Color scheme: Contrasting
Size: 35 cm. diameter
Tendency: Clustered

The groups of red candles are the keynotes here, arranged in an 8-5-3 ratio on a bed of elegant green leaves whose sober, quiet shape transforms this centerpiece into a festive classic without recourse to the ubiquitous Christmas tree. At the foot of each group of candles anthurium leaves are used to create a graphic, enveloping line.

 **Ingredients**

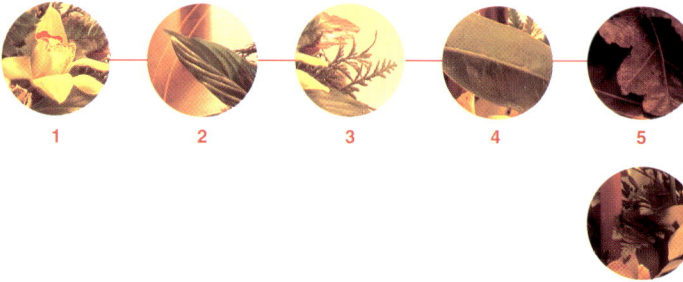

1   2   3   4   5

6

1 Cymbidium Gy Cooksbridge / Cybidium   2 Spathiphyllum kochii / Peace lily   3 Platycladus orientalis / Platycladus
4 Anthurium veitchii / Anthurium   5 Quercus robur / English oak   6 Polystichum coriaccum / Holly fern

christmas

Style: Classical / Formal
Technique: Foam
Color scheme: Contrasting
Size: 35 cm. diameter
Tendency: Bunched

The festive nature of this piece is shown by a candle, decorative balls and whimsical curls, while the artificial fruit and dried hydrangeas add wintry connotations. With its somber materials, warm colors and simple form and finish, this centerpiece is not difficult to make, and yet represents an essential element of Christmas decoration.

 **Ingredients**

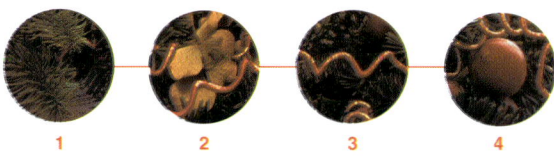

1. Abies procera / Noble fir 2. Hydrangea macrophylla / French hydrangea 3 Decorative curls
4. Red christmas balls

christmas

Style: Parallel
Technique: Foam
Color scheme: Neutral
Size: 20x15 cm.
Tendency: Units

A simple arrangement in cool colors, with base and candle in blue. Going unnoticed, avoiding glances, the will not to attract the attention of those present, is the expression of a piece containing only a handful of simple materials. Each one of these materials manages to maintain a space and character of its own: the moss with its cushion-like feel, and the pine cones with their gentle chiaroscuro.

 **Ingredients**

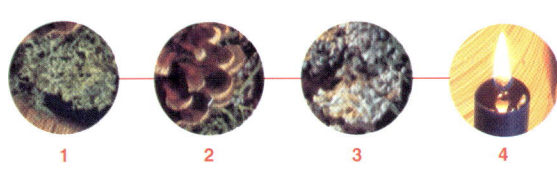

1 | 2 | 3 | 4

1 Musgo polar / Moss (treated)   2 Pine cones   3 Lichen   4 Candle

christmas

Style: Linear
Technique: Foam
Color scheme: Blue, burgundy and pink
Size: 50 cm. diameter
Tendency: Textural with flourish

The circular base is divided by an asymmetric bough, the starting point around which the clusters are arranged in an 8-5-3 ratio to avoid monotony and add texture. The hardness of the bough and the pine cones is mitigated by their combination with soft pink and blue tones, in perfect harmony with the satiny texture of the base. White stars with gold glitter, attached with coiled wire, provide the Christmas touch.

Ingredients

1. Chrysanthemum Kloindike / Chysanthemum (burgundy)   2. Hedera helix / English ivy   3. Rosa gerdo / Rose
4. Centaurea cyanus / Cornflower   5. Asparagus umbellatus midiocladus / Asparagus   6. Bough   7. Pine cones

christmas

Style: Formal
Technique: Foam
Color scheme: Contrasting
Size: 80x35 cm.
Tendency: Semitransparency

Using the most traditional of materials in classical forms with a semitransparent tendency, we obtain a centerpiece with a modern feel. A touch of gold on the edges of the rose petals adds a hint of sophistication to the whole, while at the same time countering the rustic notes of the fir and lichen on the branches.

 **Ingredients**

1. Rosa pareo / Orange rose   2. Rosa Dallas / Red rose   3. Ilex aquifolium / Holly
4. Abies procera / Fir   5. Lichen

christmas

Style: Formal
Technique: Foam
Color scheme: Monochrome
Size: 40 cm. diameter
Tendency: Units

This centerpiece is made from the sort of things you might come across on a walk in the country or round a garden, and its merit lies in the way the various homogenous materials have been put together. The whole arrangement seems to have been conceived with one purpose: to recreate the coziness of wintertime. It is charged with vitality and aroma by small eucalyptus blooms, which at the same time are redolent of winter.

 **Ingredients**

1   2   3   4   5

Spruce cone   Asparagus umbellatus midiocladus / Asparagus   Abies procera / Noble fir

Platycladus orientalis / Platycladus   Eucalyptus globolus / Cider gum (in bloom)

Style: Formal
Technique: Collage
Color scheme: Warm
Size: 40x36 cm
Tendency: Clustered

The contrast between the transparency of the decorative fabric on its rustic wreath and the irregular side cluster makes for an exquisite duality. The luxury expressed by this transparency transports one to a festive atmosphere, an elegant, sumptuous dinner followed by champagne. The compact core centers the work and provides it with a specific optical weight.

Ingredients

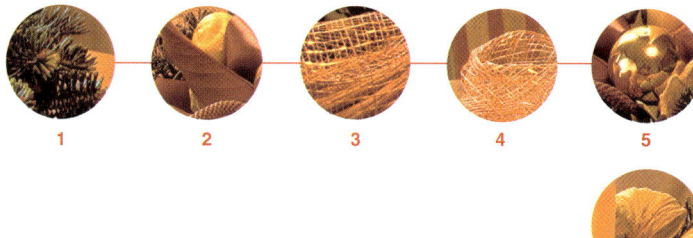

1.Abies procera / Noble fir   2.Magnolia soulangiana / Saucer magnolia (leaves)   3.Wicker wreath
4.Mesh fabric   5.Christmas balls   6.Paper bows

christmas

Style: Free
Technique: Organic structure
Color scheme: Chromatic
Size: 70x30 cm.
Tendency: Clustered

Make a wicker structure and attach it to the base with lengths of raffia. Everything is woven or tied together or suspended in such a way as to be completely stable. Whereas some of the materials are quite independent, others wrap gently round each other, creating an interplay of lines that sets the rhythms of the piece.

🌹 Ingredients

1   2   3   4   5

6

1. Salix viminalis / Common osier   2. Maranta leuconeura / Prayer plant   3. Rosa canina / Dog rose
4. Yucca gloriosa / Spanish dagger   5. Tulipa gesnerana / Tulip   6. Pine cones

Style: Decorative
Technique: Dry foam
Color scheme: Contrasting
Size: 60x48x35 cm.
Tendency: Clustered

Fill a wickerwork base to the brim with foam, ensuring that no gap is left in the middle – otherwise it will be difficult to keep the candles completely vertical. Once the central axis is properly established, mark the two ends with platycladus and corncobs respectively. Then insert the remaining elements, making sure that they are not excessively bunched. This centerpiece is the result of a balanced mixture of elegance and rusticity that can easily be adapted to any surroundings.

Ingredients

1. Zea mays / Maize (dyed corn cob)   2. Schinus molle / Pepper tree   3. Platycladus orientalis / Platycladus
4. Golden mushroom   5. Raffia (natural, dyed)   6. Hazelnuts   7. Foeniculum vulgare / Fennel

christmas

Style: Decorative asymmetric
Technique: Radial
Color scheme: Chromatic
Size: 80x55 cm.
Tendency: Stil life

A Christmas still life made entirely of natural materials of animal and plant origin. It has a rustic feel, the pheasant's elegant plumage providing great chromatic richness, and constituting the common ground between all the elements that make up the composition. Unless the pheasant is a gift, it is advisable to use a stuffed bird. The springs of pepper tree add movement to the center of the still life.

🌸 Ingredients

1   2   3   4   5

6   7   8

Schinus molle / Pepper tree (leaves and fruits)   Gerbera jamesonii hibrida / Gerbera
Passiflora caerulea / Passion flower   Prunus laurocerasus / Cherry laurel   Kingfisher
Pheasant   Pumpkins   Quinces

accessories

christmas

Style: Decorative
Technique: Layering
Color scheme: Complementary
Size: 170 cm. x 1.50 m.
Tendency: Minimalist

Cones made of medulla in the classic basketwork style comprise the main motif in this Christmas arrangement. Start at the tip and work upwards and outwards. When complete, they are used upside down in the arrangement. The matching decorations add a festive touch. A ribbon in the same tone and its complementary color is wound round to complete the composition. The result is a sober atmosphere obtained by using only a few well chosen elements of considerable size and marked personality.

 **Ingredients**

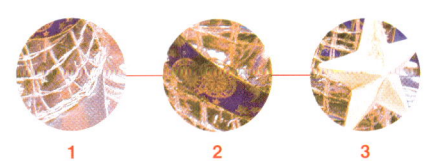

1   2   3

Cones of treated wicker   Ribbon   Decorations

Style: Christmas tree / classic piramyd
Technique: structure
Color scheme: Natural
Size: Height 50 cm.
Tendency: Woven

First make a cross out of bamboo to set the diameter of the cone shape. On top of this, place a skeleton of wire mesh molded to the correct shape and covered in newspaper. Then glue natural moss all over this structure, with the help of some rusty wire. Place the decorations in a triangular pattern. The result is a tree that is undemanding and pleasing to the eye, a composition that fits all styles and conserves the allegorical elements we expect from a Christmas decoration.

 **Ingredients**

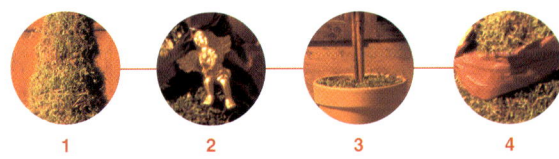

1 2 3 4

1.Musgo 2.Fantasías 3.Troncos de bambú 4.Cinta de papel

christmas

Style: Formal
Technique: Collage
Color scheme: Monochrome
Size: 30 cm.
Tendency: Woven

A piece in an innocent style, its playful, simple tone inviting even the youngest children to play a part in Christmas decorating. Reflecting this finish, choosing these colors and giving them shape are signs of artistic maturity, and the expression of a soul that preserves the virtues of childhood, that is capable of admiring simple things and enjoying beauty for its own sake, before the mind makes its mark on it.

 **Ingredients**

1 Moss (treated)   2 Pine cones   3 Lavandula angustifolia / Lavender

Style: Decorative
Technique: Wiring
Color scheme: Contrasting
Size: 15 cm.
Tendency: Clustered

The pine cones, platycladus and coiled wire, three elements with Christmas connotations, are harmonized with the lantana and integrate it into the whole. This rustic plant of gardens and sunny rookeries, both on the shores of the Mediterranean and inland, forms part of a floral language that is individually wrought, using clusters and a thoughtful selection of materials to suggest the words or nuances that one wishes to express.

 **Ingredients**

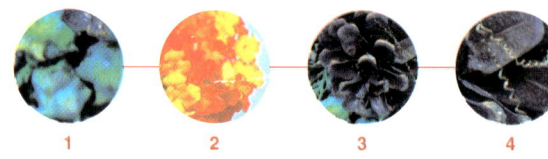

1.Platycladus orientalis / Platycladus   2.Lantana camara / Common lantana   3.Pine cones   4.Coiled metal wire

christmas

Style: Decorative
Technique: Collage
Color scheme: Warm
Size: 50x20 cm.
Tendency: Clustered

All the elements used here are artificial; this, combined with their lightness, means that all they need is to be arranged and glued. In the strong central cluster, the green of the bow and the black of the berries heighten the color contrast. The cinnamon sticks have been lightly varnished to modify their rustic look and give them a touch of elegance.

Ingredients

1   2   3   4

1 Apple (artificial)   2 Bow (paper)   3 Berries (red and black)   4 Cinnamon (varnished)

christmas

Style: Classical half-moon
Technique: Collage
Color scheme: Contrasting
Size: 150x75 cm.
Tendency: Bunched

Once the base of dry foam is covered with bunched, compact material, add loose cascades of love-lies-bleeding in contrasting colors for extra showiness. Fruits and balls form "planets" around the central figure, which is decorated with coiled wire to lend a luminous touch. Details in gold harmonize perfectly with the overall color scheme.

 **Ingredients**

1. Magnolia soulangiana / Saucer magnolia (leaves) 2. Platanus orientalis / Oriental plane (leaves)
3. Amaranthus caudatus / Love-lies-bleeding 4. Lichen 5. Golden mushroom 6. Fruits 7. Dried flowers
8. Pods

christmas

Style: Spherical shapes
Technique: Spiral
Color scheme: Whole range
Size: 30x20 cm.
Tendency: Bunched

Accessory consisting of several different arrangements using spiky shapes. While some are wired and others left with their own stems, they share the coiled wire finish, which adds a festive note. Some of the composition is short-lived, while other elements have a longer life span, and so keep the memory of the overall effect intact; it is one more way of perpetuating the pieces.

🌹 Ingredients

1. Lavender   2. Strawberries   3. Grapes   4. Litchis   5. Ribbons

christmas accessories

Style: Classical
Technique: Secured with guide
Color scheme: Monochrome
Size: 2.10 mts.
Tendency: Compact

A festoon to adorn a simple candelabrum. The ornamentation sets it off and renders it more sublime, highlighting the two ends and the center with Christmas decorations. The clusters are distributed symmetrically throughout the festoon. Its warm tones make it blend in with its surroundings, creating a pleasant overall effect. There is always a place for this kind of piece, regardless of how it is worked.

 **Ingredients**

1.Hydrangea macrophylla / French hydrangea   2.Asparagus sprengeri / Asparagus
3.Pomegranates   4.Cinnamon   5.Christmas decoration

christmas

Style: Avant-garde
Technique: Collage
Color scheme: Warm
Size: 15x15x3 cm.
Tendency: Related

Presentation and gift-wrapping have reached the point of being a minor work of art in themselves, being at times quite long-lived and sometimes more ephemeral. In this presentation for an article of jewelry, the cinnamon and its aromatic equivalent are associated in the memory, as are the rose hips with their lively, intense color. The presentation contrasts with and high-lights the contents of the box.

 **Ingredients**

1   2   3

1. Rosa canina / Dog rose   2. Cinnamon   3. Decorative wire

Style: Classical
Technique: Interwoven
Color scheme: Ranging from beige to brown
Size: Length 3 m
Tendency: Modern

The garland and the tree are in the same style, since they form a single decorative unit. Sew the materials onto a wire guide, overlapping them in a scale pattern and distributing them irregularly in order to create rhythms enlivening the composition. A semitransparent ribbon traces the route from one end to the other, while toy saucepans adorn the tree for a whimsical touch.

 **Ingredients**

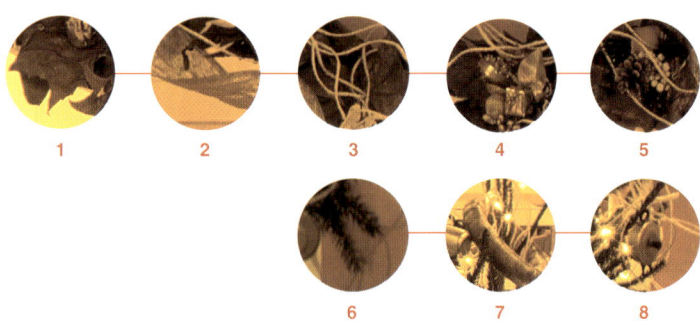

1. Platanus orientalis / Oriental plane (leaves)   2. Wired ribbon   3. Cord   4. Christmas decorations   5. Pine cones
6. Abies procera / Noble fir   7. Padded wreath   8. Toy saucepan

Editor
Josep Mª Minguet

Production and Art Director
Louis Bou

Graphic Design and Layout
Mònica Pera

Documentation and Writing
Flora Miserachs

Photography
Joan Argelés

Links International
c/ Jonqueres, 10. 1º, 5ª
08003 Barcelona
Tel. +34 93 301 21 99
Fax:+34 93 301 00 21

info@linksbooks.net
www.linksbooks.net

© **I.Monsa de Ediciones,S.A.**

ISBN: 84-89861-16-1
DL: B-10110-2003
Printed in Spain